Better is a dinner of herbs where love is, than a stalled ox and hatred therewith.

—*Proverbs* 15:17

This gift of herbs was given to

_____

by

_____

on

_____

Watercolors by Claudia Karabaic Sargent

Text by Peg Streep

VIKING
STUDIO
BOOKS

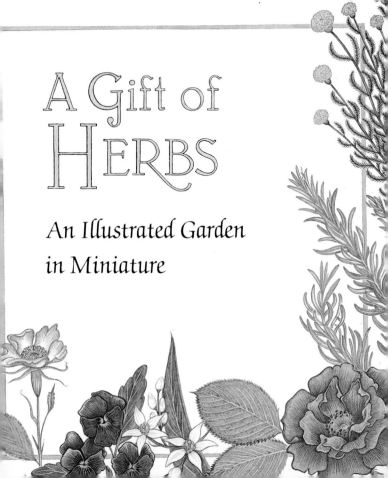

A Gift of Herbs

An Illustrated Garden in Miniature

For Frank with all my love, for always being there.
—C.K.S.

For Alexandra from Mama with love.
—P.S.

VIKING STUDIO BOOKS
Published by the Penguin Group
Viking Penguin, a division of Penguin Books USA Inc.,
375 Hudson Street, New York, New York 10014, U.S.A.
Penguin Books Ltd, 27 Wrights Lane, London W8 5TZ, England
Penguin Books Australia Ltd, Ringwood, Victoria, Australia
Penguin Books Canada Ltd, 2801 John Street, Markham, Ontario, Canada L3R 1B4
Penguin Books (N.Z.) Ltd, 182–190 Wairau Road, Auckland 10, New Zealand

Penguin Books Ltd, Registered Offices: Harmondsworth, Middlesex, England

First published in 1991 by Viking Penguin, a division of Penguin Books USA Inc.

1 3 5 7 9 10 8 6 4 2

LIBRARY OF CONGRESS CATALOGING IN PUBLICATION DATA
Streep, Peg.
A gift of herbs / Peg Streep ; illustrated by Claudia Sargent.
p.   cm.
ISBN 0-670-83452-1
1. Herbs.   2. Herbs—Utilization.   3. Herbs—Gift books.
I. Sargent, Claudia Karabaic.   II. Title.
SB351.H5S76   1991
635'.7—dc20   90-50443

Printed in Japan   Set in Zapf Chancery Medium 10% Condensed

A PROMISED LAND PRODUCTION

The English word "herb" comes from the Latin *herba*, for "green crops" or "grass." In its broadest definition, an herb is any plant without a woody stem, but for most of us the word evokes tastes, smells, and sights: the surprising pepper flavor of the delicate nasturtium; the vivid pungency of a sprig of rosemary; the cool taste of dill; the heady scent of the rose; the visual elegance of the sunflower and the crack of its seed between the teeth.

Herbs continue to delight. The properties and myths ascribed to them give these plants a special luster and remind us that they have held a primary place in human life for centuries. Rediscovering that ancient history lends a special magic to the herbs we find all around us in our contemporary world.

The herbs in this gift have been chosen for their beauty, their taste, and their history. While they are in the main culinary herbs, we've included some others that are dear to us. All are listed alphabetically, but you will find special pages devoted to herbal topics scattered throughout, and since many of the illustrated borders contain more than one herb, we have included a key to the art on the last pages.

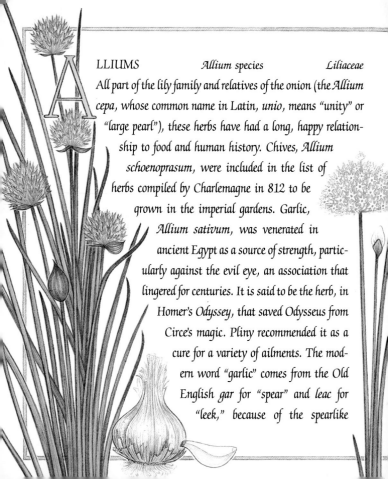

ALLIUMS   *Allium* species   Liliaceae

All part of the lily family and relatives of the onion (the *Allium cepa*, whose common name in Latin, *unio*, means "unity" or "large pearl"), these herbs have had a long, happy relationship to food and human history. Chives, *Allium schoenoprasum*, were included in the list of herbs compiled by Charlemagne in 812 to be grown in the imperial gardens. Garlic, *Allium sativum*, was venerated in ancient Egypt as a source of strength, particularly against the evil eye, an association that lingered for centuries. It is said to be the herb, in Homer's *Odyssey*, that saved Odysseus from Circe's magic. Pliny recommended it as a cure for a variety of ailments. The modern word "garlic" comes from the Old English *gar* for "spear" and *leac* for "leek," because of the spearlike shape of the plant's leaves. The Chinese, or garlic, chive, *Allium tuberosum*, was first used by the Chinese thousands of years ago.

Leek, *Allium porrum*, was eaten by Nero, who used it to clear his voice; it later became the symbol of Wales, celebrating, some say, an ancient victory of the Celts over the Saxons. The shallot, *Allium ascalonicum*, is the mildest and most delicate of the family. "Scallion" is a common term for the young, not fully developed bulb of the shallot or leek. Most of us would ally ourselves with Chaucer's Summoner, of whom it was said in *The Canterbury Tales*, "Wel loved he garleek, oynons, and eek lekes."

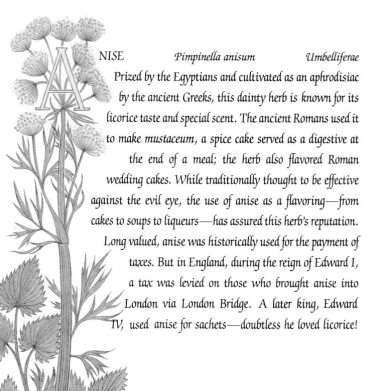

ANISE *Pimpinella anisum* *Umbelliferae*

Prized by the Egyptians and cultivated as an aphrodisiac by the ancient Greeks, this dainty herb is known for its licorice taste and special scent. The ancient Romans used it to make *mustaceum*, a spice cake served as a digestive at the end of a meal; the herb also flavored Roman wedding cakes. While traditionally thought to be effective against the evil eye, the use of anise as a flavoring—from cakes to soups to liqueurs—has assured this herb's reputation. Long valued, anise was historically used for the payment of taxes. But in England, during the reign of Edward I, a tax was levied on those who brought anise into London via London Bridge. A later king, Edward IV, used anise for sachets—doubtless he loved licorice!

BASIL *Ocimum basilicum* *Labiatae*

The ancient Greeks called it *basilicum*, or "royal plant," but when the Romans renamed it, they confused its heritage with *basiliscus*, the basilisk, the legendary reptile whose breath and look were fatal. The latter association stayed with the herb for centuries, for, as William Turner commented in 1562, "Basil . . . is good for the striking of the sea dragon." By 1597, John Gerard in his *Herball* had given the royal plant its due, writing that "the smell of Basil is good for the heart . . . it taketh away sorrowfulness, which cometh of melancholy, and maketh a man merry and glade." Oddly, while in the Language of Flowers basil signified hatred, in many countries it has a tradition as a love token and a symbol of romance. Pots of it were sometimes given as tokens of affection.

B

AY — *Laurus nobilis* — Lauraceae

Bay, the most celebrated and noble of herbs (as its species name, *nobilis*, tells us), was sacred to Apollo, the Greek Olympian god associated with prophecy, medicine, music, and poetry. The Delphic priestesses prophesied with a bay leaf between their lips, while laurel crowned victors and poets alike. Its leaf was thought to ward off pestilence and contagion.

In later centuries, bay garnered other associations. It was thought, from Roman times forward, to protect against the forces of nature and later the unnatural as well. The seventeenth-century herbalist Nicholas Culpeper reported that it was potent against witchcraft, and that "neither witch nor devil, thunder nor lightening will hurt a man where bay is." The withering of laurel was an omen of death, and a superstition that the trees would die before the death or fall of a king persisted from the time of the Roman Empire and was still current when Shakespeare mentioned it in *Richard II*.

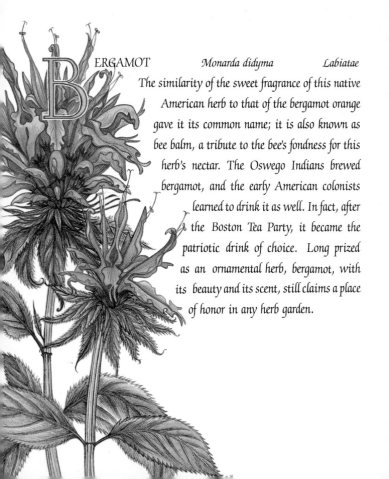

BERGAMOT

Monarda didyma   *Labiatae*

The similarity of the sweet fragrance of this native American herb to that of the bergamot orange gave it its common name; it is also known as bee balm, a tribute to the bee's fondness for this herb's nectar. The Oswego Indians brewed bergamot, and the early American colonists learned to drink it as well. In fact, after the Boston Tea Party, it became the patriotic drink of choice. Long prized as an ornamental herb, bergamot, with its beauty and its scent, still claims a place of honor in any herb garden.

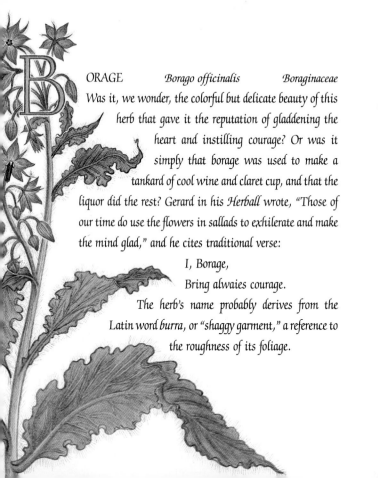

BORAGE   *Borago officinalis*   *Boraginaceae*

Was it, we wonder, the colorful but delicate beauty of this herb that gave it the reputation of gladdening the heart and instilling courage? Or was it simply that borage was used to make a tankard of cool wine and claret cup, and that the liquor did the rest? Gerard in his *Herball* wrote, "Those of our time do use the flowers in sallads to exhilerate and make the mind glad," and he cites traditional verse:

> I, Borage,
> Bring alwaies courage.

The herb's name probably derives from the Latin word *burra*, or "shaggy garment," a reference to the roughness of its foliage.

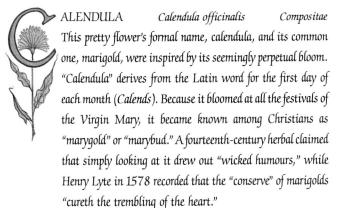

CALENDULA *Calendula officinalis* *Compositae*

This pretty flower's formal name, calendula, and its common one, marigold, were inspired by its seemingly perpetual bloom. "Calendula" derives from the Latin word for the first day of each month (*Calends*). Because it bloomed at all the festivals of the Virgin Mary, it became known among Christians as "marygold" or "marybud." A fourteenth-century herbal claimed that simply looking at it drew out "wicked humours," while Henry Lyte in 1578 recorded that the "conserve" of marigolds "cureth the trembling of the heart."

Calendula was so popular as a flavoring and food coloring for stews and soups that it also was known as "pot marigold" but its charms never dimmed. John Keats wrote:

> Open afresh your round of starry folds,
> Ye ardent marigolds!
> Dry up the moisture from your golden lids,
> For great Apollo bids
> That in these days your praises should be sung. . . .

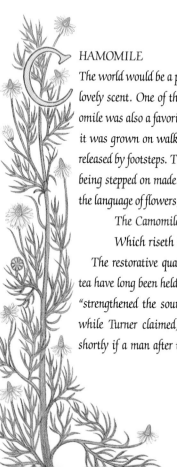

CHAMOMILE *Matricaria recutita* *Compositae*

The world would be a poorer place without this herb—and its lovely scent. One of the most popular of folk remedies, chamomile was also a favorite strewing herb in the Middle Ages—it was grown on walks in gardens so that its scent would be released by footsteps. The herb's characteristic rising even after being stepped on made it a symbol of "energy in adversity" in the language of flowers; as a seventeenth-century writer put it,

> The Camomile shall teach thee patience
> Which riseth best when trodden most upon.

The restorative qualities of chamomile when brewed as a tea have long been held: John Parkinson in 1656 wrote that it "strengthened the sound" and "eased pain in the deseased," while Turner claimed, "It will restore a man to hys color shortly if a man after the longe use of the bathe drynke it."

CORIANDER   *Coriandrum sativum*   Umbelliferae

One of the most ancient of all herbs—known to the Egyptians, Greeks, and Romans as a spice and medicine—coriander was thought by the Chinese to confer immortality. Mentioned in both Exodus and Numbers, it is one of the bitter herbs used in the Passover ceremony.

Coriander's pungent odor has discouraged some herbalists. Pliny named it *coriandrum* from the Greek word for "bug" (*koris*), while Gerard in his herbal called it "a very stinking herbe." In fact, the striking difference between the odor of the fresh plant and the fragrance of the dried seed gave coriander its meaning in the Victorian Language of Flowers: "hidden merit." Once touted as an aphrodisiac, this herb has earned its niche in the culinary world, particularly in the cuisines of India and the Far East.

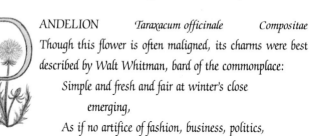

DANDELION   *Taraxacum officinale*   *Compositae*

Though this flower is often maligned, its charms were best described by Walt Whitman, bard of the commonplace:

> Simple and fresh and fair at winter's close
>> emerging,
> As if no artifice of fashion, business, politics,
>> had ever been,
> Forth from its sunny nook of shelter'd
>> grass—innocent, golden, calm as the dawn,
> The spring's first dandelion shows its trustful face.

Despite its humble origins, the dandelion has a long medicinal history in cultures as various as those of Arabia and India, as well as in continental Europe. The jagged edges of the leaves of the herb gave it its name—from the French "lion's tooth," or *dent de lion*. What the dandelion lacks in sumptuousness and rarity, it makes up for in luscious treats: the young greens make a delicious salad, while the flowers yield a potent country libation, dandelion wine.

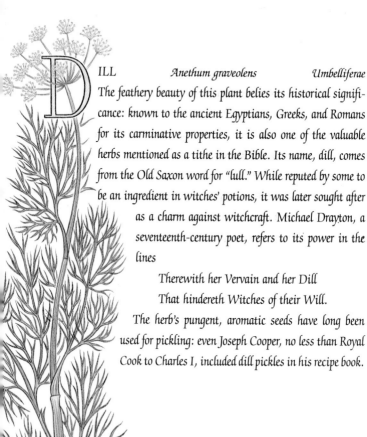

DILL

Anethum graveolens   *Umbelliferae*

The feathery beauty of this plant belies its historical significance: known to the ancient Egyptians, Greeks, and Romans for its carminative properties, it is also one of the valuable herbs mentioned as a tithe in the Bible. Its name, dill, comes from the Old Saxon word for "lull." While reputed by some to be an ingredient in witches' potions, it was later sought after as a charm against witchcraft. Michael Drayton, a seventeenth-century poet, refers to its power in the lines

> Therewith her Vervain and her Dill
> That hindereth Witches of their Will.

The herb's pungent, aromatic seeds have long been used for pickling: even Joseph Cooper, no less than Royal Cook to Charles I, included dill pickles in his recipe book.

L avender's blue, dilly dilly, lavender's green,

When I am King, dilly dilly, you shall be Queen.

Who told you so, dilly dilly, who told you so?

'Twas my own heart, dilly dilly, that told me so.

—TRADITIONAL

FENNEL   *Foeniculum vulgare*   *Umbelliferae*

It's no accident that when John Milton, writing *Paradise Lost*, described the scents of Eden, this wonderful herb came to mind:

> When from the boughs a savory odor blown,
> Grateful to appetite, more pleas'd my sense
> Than smell of sweetest Fennel. . . .

Known to the Greeks and Romans alike, fennel was considered a plant of many virtues, good for everything from restoring eyesight to giving courage and strength, and was also given as a reward for achievement.

In folklore, fennel had spiritual properties as well. A charm from the tenth century against evil spirits lists fennel as one of the nine sacred herbs that "have power against nine magic outcasts, against nine flying things, against the loathèd things that over land rove." In the Middle Ages, doors were decorated with fennel to ward off Midsummer Eve spirits, and fennel was included in the Sabbath posy, the collection of herbs carried to church.

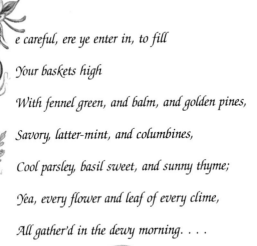

*B*e careful, ere ye enter in, to fill

Your baskets high

With fennel green, and balm, and golden pines,

Savory, latter-mint, and columbines,

Cool parsley, basil sweet, and sunny thyme;

Yea, every flower and leaf of every clime,

All gather'd in the dewy morning. . . .

—JOHN KEATS

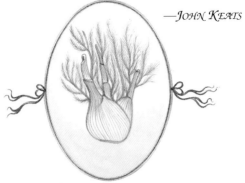

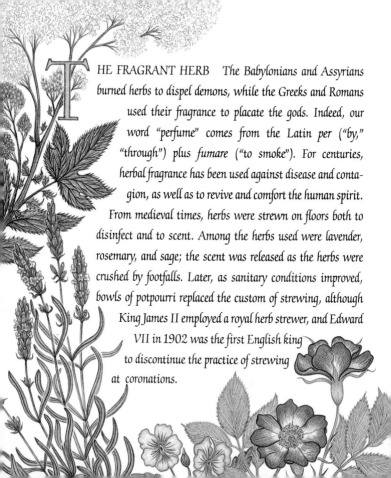

THE FRAGRANT HERB The Babylonians and Assyrians burned herbs to dispel demons, while the Greeks and Romans used their fragrance to placate the gods. Indeed, our word "perfume" comes from the Latin *per* ("by," "through") plus *fumare* ("to smoke"). For centuries, herbal fragrance has been used against disease and contagion, as well as to revive and comfort the human spirit. From medieval times, herbs were strewn on floors both to disinfect and to scent. Among the herbs used were lavender, rosemary, and sage; the scent was released as the herbs were crushed by footfalls. Later, as sanitary conditions improved, bowls of potpourri replaced the custom of strewing, although King James II employed a royal herb strewer, and Edward VII in 1902 was the first English king to discontinue the practice of strewing at coronations.

While the poor held sprigs of herbs to their noses in the streets, those better off used pomanders to scent and protect. The word "pomander" comes from the French *pomme*, or "apple," in reference to the shape, and *ambre*, possibly a shortened form of *ambregris*, which is a fixative for perfume. Pomanders were originally cases for scent, worn from the neck or waist and made of a variety of metals or wood. They were often exchanged as love tokens, as these lines from Robert Herrick, a seventeenth-century poet, attest:

> To me my Julia lately sent
> A Bracelet richly Redolent.
> The Beads I kist, but most lov'd her
> That did   perfume the Pomander.

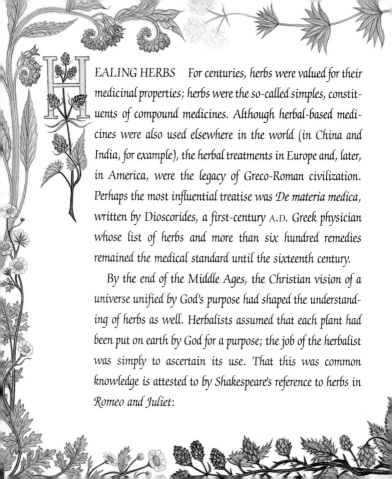

HEALING HERBS   For centuries, herbs were valued for their medicinal properties; herbs were the so-called simples, constituents of compound medicines. Although herbal-based medicines were also used elsewhere in the world (in China and India, for example), the herbal treatments in Europe and, later, in America, were the legacy of Greco-Roman civilization. Perhaps the most influential treatise was *De materia medica*, written by Dioscorides, a first-century A.D. Greek physician whose list of herbs and more than six hundred remedies remained the medical standard until the sixteenth century.

By the end of the Middle Ages, the Christian vision of a universe unified by God's purpose had shaped the understanding of herbs as well. Herbalists assumed that each plant had been put on earth by God for a purpose; the job of the herbalist was simply to ascertain its use. That this was common knowledge is attested to by Shakespeare's reference to herbs in *Romeo and Juliet*:

O! mickle is the powerful grace that lies

In Herbs, plants, stones, and their true qualities:

For nought so vile that on the earth doth live

But to the earth some special good doth give.

To this, Paracelsus, a sixteenth-century physician and alchemist, added the "Doctrine of Signatures": the theory that a plant's "signature"—how it looked—indicated how it could be used. This view long informed (or, better put, misinformed) the use of healing herbs: thus it was thought that a yellow herb could cure jaundice, while a red rose could cure nosebleeds. The heart shape of certain pansies was thought to indicate that it would be beneficial to heart ailments. Many common herbal names—lungwort and feverfew, for example—reflect their "signatures."

Before modern synthetic drugs, all medicines were herbal. Herbs are powerful: some are poisonous, while others may prove harmful when consumed in large quantities. No herbal remedy should be taken without the guidance of a health professional or a physician.

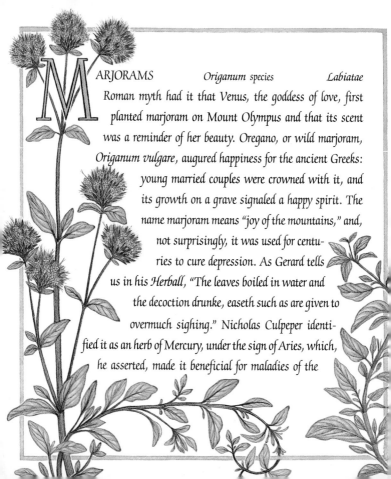

MARJORAMS   *Origanum* species   *Labiatae*

Roman myth had it that Venus, the goddess of love, first planted marjoram on Mount Olympus and that its scent was a reminder of her beauty. Oregano, or wild marjoram, *Origanum vulgare*, augured happiness for the ancient Greeks: young married couples were crowned with it, and its growth on a grave signaled a happy spirit. The name marjoram means "joy of the mountains," and, not surprisingly, it was used for centuries to cure depression. As Gerard tells us in his *Herball*, "The leaves boiled in water and the decoction drunke, easeth such as are given to overmuch sighing." Nicholas Culpeper identified it as an herb of Mercury, under the sign of Aries, which, he asserted, made it beneficial for maladies of the brain. Sweet marjoram, *Origanum majorana*, was used for its sweet perfume in the bath, as a strewing herb, and in nosegays. An old English superstition maintained that rubbing a sprig of sweet marjoram mixed with marigold flowers, thyme, and wormwood, ground to a powder, and then simmered with other ingredients, on a young girl's head on St. Luke's Day would permit her to dream of her future husband. In the same vein, in the Victorian Language of Flowers, marjoram stood for blushes. All of the marjorams are pretty plants, whose sight alone is enough to cheer the heart, but especially golden marjoram, *Origanum vulgare* 'Aureum.' Beauty aside, these herbs are the favorites of many a cook.

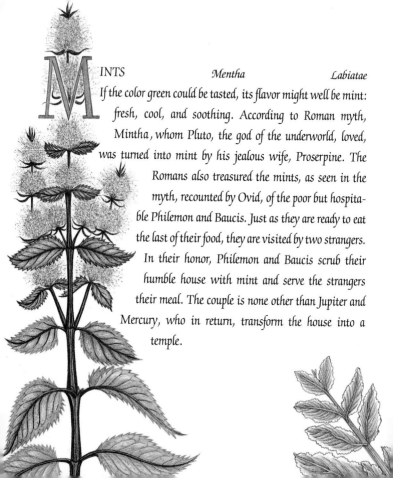

MINTS

Mentha   *Labiatae*

If the color green could be tasted, its flavor might well be mint: fresh, cool, and soothing. According to Roman myth, Mintha, whom Pluto, the god of the underworld, loved, was turned into mint by his jealous wife, Proserpine. The Romans also treasured the mints, as seen in the myth, recounted by Ovid, of the poor but hospitable Philemon and Baucis. Just as they are ready to eat the last of their food, they are visited by two strangers. In their honor, Philemon and Baucis scrub their humble house with mint and serve the strangers their meal. The couple is none other than Jupiter and Mercury, who in return, transform the house into a temple.

Long used in baths and tisanes to relax and soothe, mint
has a scent that, as Turner says in his herbal, "rejoiceth
the heart of man." In later centuries, the mints gained
popularity as medicinal herbs, most of them drunk as
teas. In modern times, mint is used largely as a flavoring, both in the home and commercially.

Because the species interbreed, they are often hard to
distinguish, but the types shown here are peppermint,
apple mint, spearmint, and pennyroyal.

MUSTARD   *Brassica nigra*   Cruciferae

The earliest history of mustard is medicinal: the herb's importance convinced the ancient Greeks that Asclepius, one of the sons of Apollo and the god of healing, had discovered it. The Romans used it medicinally, but also introduced it as a condiment. Pliny, in his *Natural History*, commented that the pungency of mustard burned but that it was "remarkably wholesome for the body" and listed some forty remedies that included mustard. The herb's name derives from the Latin words *mustum*, referring to the unfermented wine with which mustard seeds were mixed, and *ardens*, or "burning."

Centuries later, English herbalists still esteemed mustard: John Evelyn thought it "quickened and revived the spirit," while Nicholas Culpeper held it cured everything from the "malignity of mushrooms" to toothaches, hair loss, bruises, and "the crick in the neck."

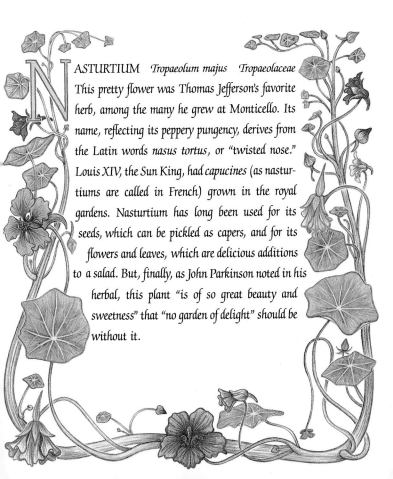

NASTURTIUM *Tropaeolum majus* *Tropaeolaceae*
This pretty flower was Thomas Jefferson's favorite
herb, among the many he grew at Monticello. Its
name, reflecting its peppery pungency, derives from
the Latin words *nasus tortus*, or "twisted nose."
Louis XIV, the Sun King, had *capucines* (as nastur-
tiums are called in French) grown in the royal
gardens. Nasturtium has long been used for its
seeds, which can be pickled as capers, and for its
flowers and leaves, which are delicious additions
to a salad. But, finally, as John Parkinson noted in his
herbal, this plant "is of so great beauty and
sweetness" that "no garden of delight" should be
without it.

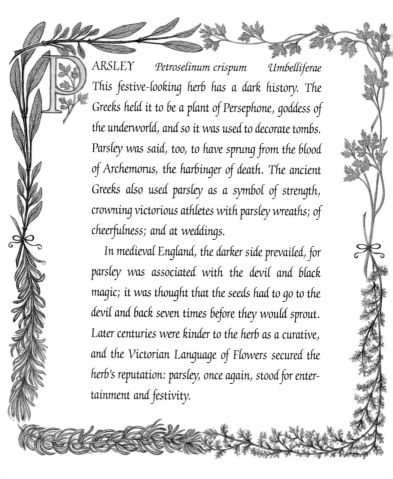

PARSLEY   *Petroselinum crispum*   *Umbelliferae*

This festive-looking herb has a dark history. The Greeks held it to be a plant of Persephone, goddess of the underworld, and so it was used to decorate tombs. Parsley was said, too, to have sprung from the blood of Archemorus, the harbinger of death. The ancient Greeks also used parsley as a symbol of strength, crowning victorious athletes with parsley wreaths; of cheerfulness; and at weddings.

In medieval England, the darker side prevailed, for parsley was associated with the devil and black magic; it was thought that the seeds had to go to the devil and back seven times before they would sprout. Later centuries were kinder to the herb as a curative, and the Victorian Language of Flowers secured the herb's reputation: parsley, once again, stood for entertainment and festivity.

Are you going to Scarborough Fair?

Sing parsley, sage, rosemary, and thyme.

Remember me to one who lives there

For once she was a true love of mine.

Tell her to buy me an acre of land.

Sing parsley, sage, rosemary, and thyme.

Beneath the wild ocean and yonder sea strand,

And she shall be a true love of mine.

—TRADITIONAL

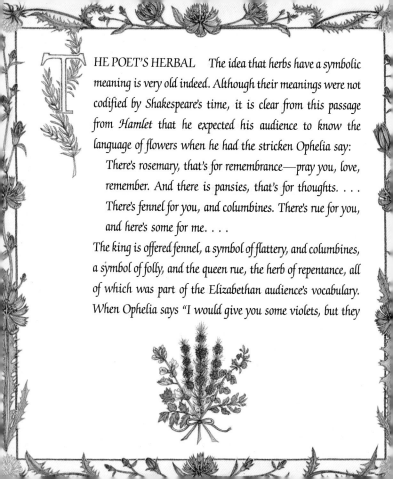

THE POET'S HERBAL   The idea that herbs have a symbolic meaning is very old indeed. Although their meanings were not codified by Shakespeare's time, it is clear from this passage from *Hamlet* that he expected his audience to know the language of flowers when he had the stricken Ophelia say:

> There's rosemary, that's for remembrance—pray you, love, remember. And there is pansies, that's for thoughts. . . .
> There's fennel for you, and columbines. There's rue for you, and here's some for me. . . .

The king is offered fennel, a symbol of flattery, and columbines, a symbol of folly, and the queen rue, the herb of repentance, all of which was part of the Elizabethan audience's vocabulary. When Ophelia says "I would give you some violets, but they withered all when my father died," the flower's meaning of faithfulness is crucial to the scene.

By the nineteenth century, the language of flowers in England had been popularized by books and standardized. Following is a list of herbs and their meanings:

basil: hatred

borage: bluntness, courage

calendula: mental anguish

chamomile: energy in
   adversity

dandelion: oracle

marjoram: blushes

mint: virtue

mustard seed: indifference

nasturtium: patriotism

rose: love

saffron crocus: mirth

sage: domestic virtue

sorrel: affection

sunflower: false riches

thyme: activity

violet (blue): faithfulness

violet (sweet): modesty

ROSE

Rosa species   *Rosaceae*

In ancient Egypt, the rose was sacred to Isis; in ancient Greece, it was part of the cult of Aphrodite. Few would disagree with the poet Sappho, who, in 600 B.C., declared it the "queen of flowers." The shield of Achilles in Homer's *Iliad* is decorated with roses. The Romans cultivated roses on a grand scale and forced the flowers to bloom throughout the year. Diners at banquets reclined on fragrant petals, and that master of excess, Nero, is said to have spent four million sesterces (a most considerable sum) on roses for a single feast. When roses were scattered or a single rose suspended above the table, all that transpired thereafter was to be kept secret, whence the expression *sub rosa* ("under the rose").

The Roman passion for roses convinced the early Christians that the flower was a pagan symbol, but even the tenets of the early church fathers (who forbade the wearing of roses) couldn't hold out against the flower's seductive charms. An emblem of Mary, the red rose came to symbolize martyrdom, and the white rose, purity.

A rose is sweeter in the bud than full-blown.

—JOHN LYLY

What's in a name? That which we call a rose

By any other name would smell as sweet.

—WILLIAM SHAKESPEARE

The Rainbow comes and goes,

And lovely is the Rose.

—WILLIAM WORDSWORTH

ROSEMARY

Rosmarinus officinalis   Labiatae

The name rosemary derives from the Latin *ros maris*, or "sea dew," because the herb grew near the sea, but it was long thought that the *maris* referred to the Virgin Mary. Legend held that when Mary and her child fled into Egypt, rosemary bushes parted to give them safe haven. When Mary spread her cloak over the bushes, their white flowers turned blue in her honor. The earliest English herbal, published in 1525, reported the tradition that the rosemary bush could grow no taller than the height Christ had attained while on earth.

This pretty, pungent herb long played a role in man's most important ceremonies. Thought by the ancients to be an aid to memory, it became a symbol of remembrance and was used at weddings, funerals, and even the celebration of Christmas. English literature abounds with references to rosemary. Sir Thomas More wrote, "I . . . lett it runne all over my garden walls, not onlie because my bees love it, but because it is the herb sacred to remembrance and, therefore, to friendship."

SAFFRON *Crocus sativus* *Iridaceae*

Saffron, which is the harvested stigmas of the *Crocus sativus*, a plant native to Asia Minor, has been the most precious of herbs for centuries, and also the most expensive, since some four thousand flowers are needed to yield one ounce of it. Saffron was known to the Greeks and Romans, who admired its color, its perfume, and its flavor. They used it to dye royal garments and even hair. Homer described the morning as saffron colored, while the Song of Solomon includes it as a scent. It is said that King Henry VIII, a man of luxury and somewhat excessive appetites, liked the flavor of saffron so much that he forbade the ladies of his court to use it as a hair dye.

SAGE   *Salvia officinalis*   Labiatae

The herb's common name means "wise," but the genus name *Salvia* comes from the Latin word *salveo*, meaning "to be well" or "in good health," a reference to this herb's long reputation as a curative. For centuries, sage was thought to heal and to render men immortal; the Latin motto *Cur moriatur homo cui Salvia crescit in horto?*—"Why should a man die when sage grows in his garden?"—was held to be true. The motto's English cousin, in turn, held that

He that would live for aye,

Must eat Sage in May.

These claims aside, the herb's culinary virtues are numerous, and in its many varieties sage adds beauty and luster to any herb garden.

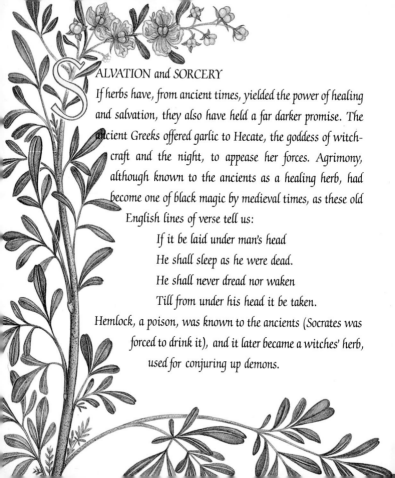

SALVATION and SORCERY

If herbs have, from ancient times, yielded the power of healing and salvation, they also have held a far darker promise. The ancient Greeks offered garlic to Hecate, the goddess of witchcraft and the night, to appease her forces. Agrimony, although known to the ancients as a healing herb, had become one of black magic by medieval times, as these old English lines of verse tell us:

> If it be laid under man's head
> He shall sleep as he were dead.
> He shall never dread nor waken
> Till from under his head it be taken.

Hemlock, a poison, was known to the ancients (Socrates was forced to drink it), and it later became a witches' herb, used for conjuring up demons.

Other herbs, though, offered protection against the dark forces. Angelica was said to be powerful against witches, evil spirits, spells, and enchantments, as the name suggests. It was believed to bloom on the day of Michael the Archangel. Saint-John's-wort was, from ancient times onward, believed to ward off spirits by the power of its scent alone, which would send them into flight. Rue was considered an anti-magic herb in Greco-Roman times; in Christian history, it became the herb of grace and repentance, in part because brushes of rue were used to sprinkle the holy water during High Mass. Rue was also said to give the gift of second sight. For protection against fairies, foxglove, another poison, was held in high esteem: it was said that the juice of the herb could return a child kidnapped by fairies.

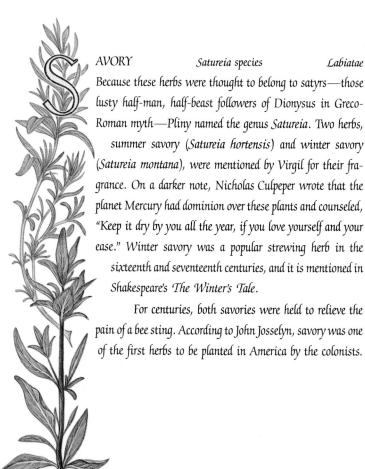

SAVORY   *Satureia* species   *Labiatae*

Because these herbs were thought to belong to satyrs—those lusty half-man, half-beast followers of Dionysus in Greco-Roman myth—Pliny named the genus *Satureia*. Two herbs, summer savory (*Satureia hortensis*) and winter savory (*Satureia montana*), were mentioned by Virgil for their fragrance. On a darker note, Nicholas Culpeper wrote that the planet Mercury had dominion over these plants and counseled, "Keep it dry by you all the year, if you love yourself and your ease." Winter savory was a popular strewing herb in the sixteenth and seventeenth centuries, and it is mentioned in Shakespeare's *The Winter's Tale*.

For centuries, both savories were held to relieve the pain of a bee sting. According to John Josselyn, savory was one of the first herbs to be planted in America by the colonists.

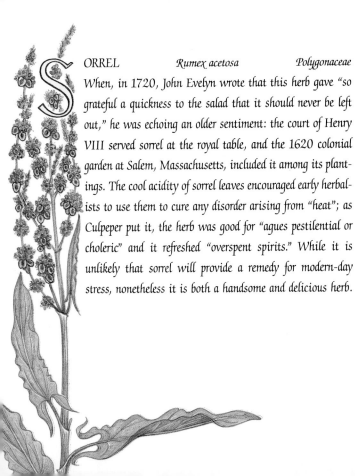

SORREL   *Rumex acetosa*   *Polygonaceae*

When, in 1720, John Evelyn wrote that this herb gave "so grateful a quickness to the salad that it should never be left out," he was echoing an older sentiment: the court of Henry VIII served sorrel at the royal table, and the 1620 colonial garden at Salem, Massachusetts, included it among its plantings. The cool acidity of sorrel leaves encouraged early herbalists to use them to cure any disorder arising from "heat"; as Culpeper put it, the herb was good for "agues pestilential or choleric" and it refreshed "overspent spirits." While it is unlikely that sorrel will provide a remedy for modern-day stress, nonetheless it is both a handsome and delicious herb.

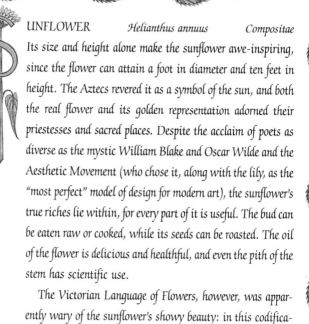

S UNFLOWER   *Helianthus annuus*   *Compositae*

Its size and height alone make the sunflower awe-inspiring, since the flower can attain a foot in diameter and ten feet in height. The Aztecs revered it as a symbol of the sun, and both the real flower and its golden representation adorned their priestesses and sacred places. Despite the acclaim of poets as diverse as the mystic William Blake and Oscar Wilde and the Aesthetic Movement (who chose it, along with the lily, as the "most perfect" model of design for modern art), the sunflower's true riches lie within, for every part of it is useful. The bud can be eaten raw or cooked, while its seeds can be roasted. The oil of the flower is delicious and healthful, and even the pith of the stem has scientific use.

The Victorian Language of Flowers, however, was apparently wary of the sunflower's showy beauty: in this codification, the sunflower stood for false riches.

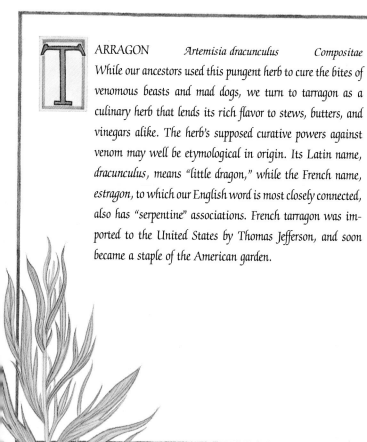

TARRAGON   *Artemisia dracunculus*   *Compositae*

While our ancestors used this pungent herb to cure the bites of venomous beasts and mad dogs, we turn to tarragon as a culinary herb that lends its rich flavor to stews, butters, and vinegars alike. The herb's supposed curative powers against venom may well be etymological in origin. Its Latin name, *dracunculus*, means "little dragon," while the French name, *estragon*, to which our English word is most closely connected, also has "serpentine" associations. French tarragon was imported to the United States by Thomas Jefferson, and soon became a staple of the American garden.

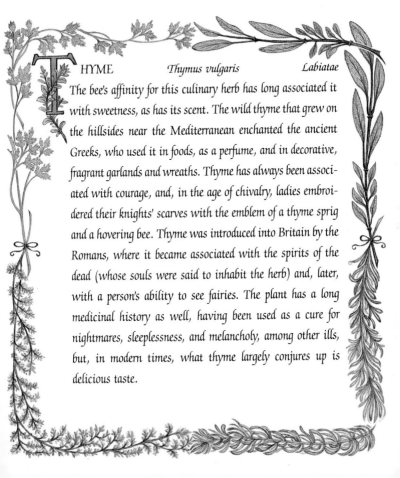

THYME

Thymus vulgaris   *Labiatae*

The bee's affinity for this culinary herb has long associated it with sweetness, as has its scent. The wild thyme that grew on the hillsides near the Mediterranean enchanted the ancient Greeks, who used it in foods, as a perfume, and in decorative, fragrant garlands and wreaths. Thyme has always been associated with courage, and, in the age of chivalry, ladies embroidered their knights' scarves with the emblem of a thyme sprig and a hovering bee. Thyme was introduced into Britain by the Romans, where it became associated with the spirits of the dead (whose souls were said to inhabit the herb) and, later, with a person's ability to see fairies. The plant has a long medicinal history as well, having been used as a cure for nightmares, sleeplessness, and melancholy, among other ills, but, in modern times, what thyme largely conjures up is delicious taste.

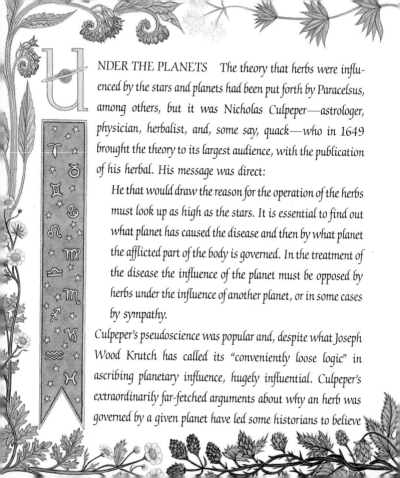

UNDER THE PLANETS The theory that herbs were influenced by the stars and planets had been put forth by Paracelsus, among others, but it was Nicholas Culpeper—astrologer, physician, herbalist, and, some say, quack—who in 1649 brought the theory to its largest audience, with the publication of his herbal. His message was direct:

> He that would draw the reason for the operation of the herbs must look up as high as the stars. It is essential to find out what planet has caused the disease and then by what planet the afflicted part of the body is governed. In the treatment of the disease the influence of the planet must be opposed by herbs under the influence of another planet, or in some cases by sympathy.

Culpeper's pseudoscience was popular and, despite what Joseph Wood Krutch has called its "conveniently loose logic" in ascribing planetary influence, hugely influential. Culpeper's extraordinarily far-fetched arguments about why an herb was governed by a given planet have led some historians to believe that he must have been writing tongue in cheek, while others, less patient, have simply labeled him a quack.

Without comment, but for fun and delectation, here is an abbreviated list of herbs, drawn from Culpeper, with their planets:

basil: Mars

bay: the sun

borage: Jupiter

dandelion: Jupiter

dill: Mercury

fennel: Mercury

marjoram: Mercury

mustard: Mars

parsley: Mercury

rose: Venus

rosemary: the sun

saffron: the sun

sage: Jupiter

savory: Mercury

thyme: Venus

violet: Venus

VIOLET

Viola odorata   *Violaceae*

This dainty flower was held dear by the ancients. In Greek myth, when Zeus turned Io into a heifer to protect her from Hera's rage, he gave her pastures of violets to eat, while in Homer's *Odyssey* the meadows of Calypso's island grew thick with violets and parsley. The flower was the emblem of ancient Athens, adorning its altars, statues, and homes. For the Romans, the violet was a symbol of modesty and purity, and bunches were strewn over the graves of children. Some vestige of that old tradition might well have inspired Shakespeare in *Hamlet*. As the dead Ophelia is borne off, Laertes declares, "And from her fair and unpolluted flesh / May violets spring!"

When the exiled Napoleon promised that he would return when the violets bloomed, his followers referred to him, in secret code, as "Monsieur Violette."

The Victorian Language of Flowers endows the fragile violet with weighty significance: it stands for faithfulness.

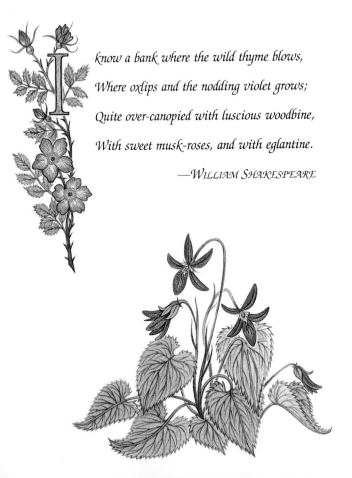

I know a bank where the wild thyme blows,

Where oxlips and the nodding violet grows;

Quite over-canopied with luscious woodbine,

With sweet musk-roses, and with eglantine.

—WILLIAM SHAKESPEARE

pend a little more time and travell in these delights of herbes and flowers . . .

—JOHN PARKINSON

In addition to the thirty-eight herbs shown and identified, other herbs are pictured in the borders and double-page spreads. What follows is a key to those herbs, reading left to right in all cases but one:

thyme corners: quotation page
columbine: initial on quotation page
Rosa rugosa alba, Rosa rugosa 'Scabrosa,' Rosa canina, Rosa nitida: dedication
sage: border of bay
chicory: border of dandelion
lavender: facing dill
columbine: facing fennel

meadowsweet, lavender, yellow violet, eglantine rose, pur-
ple violet, orange blossom, damask rose, rosemary,
santolina: "The Fragrant Herb"

comfrey, sweet woodruff, feverfew, hops (read clockwise):
"The Healing Herb," hops behind initial

parsley, sage, rosemary, and thyme: border facing parsley

rosemary, marshmallow, hyssop, horehound, rue, valerian,
mullein: "The Poet's Herbal"

Rosa rugosa: initial facing rose

rue, foxglove: "Salvation and Sorcery"

eglantine rose: initial facing violet

The endpapers of this book depict nasturtium. Pictured on
the jacket are meadowsweet, chives, spearmint, dandelion,
rosemary, tarragon, bay, rose, dill, parsley, chamomile, and
lavender.